LET'S RIDE!

MONSTER TRUCKS

MARIE ROGERS

PowerKiDS
press

NEW YORK

Published in 2022 by The Rosen Publishing Group, Inc.
29 East 21st Street, New York, NY 10010

First Edition

Portions of this work were originally authored by J. Poolos and published as *Wild About Monster Trucks*. All new material this edition authored by Marie Rogers.

Editor: Kate Mikoley
Book Design: Rachel Rising

Photo Credits: Cover yackers1/Shutterstock.com; Cover, pp. 1, 3, 4, 6, 8, 10, 12, 14, 16, 18, 20, 22, 23, 24 StarLine/Shutterstock.com; Cover, p.1 absemetov/Shutterstock.com; p. 4 MR1805/iStock/Getty Images Plus; pp. 5, 8, 17 FAYEZ NURELDINE/Staff/AFP/Getty Images; pp. 6, 7 NurPhoto/Contributor/Getty Images; p. 9 Ronald C. Modra/Contributor/Getty Images Sport/Getty Images; p. 11 Tim DeFrisco/Stringer/Getty Images Sport/Getty Images; p. 12 SOPA Images/Contributor/LightRocket/Getty Images; p. 13 Chris Ryan - Corbis/Contributor/Corbis Sport/Getty Images; p. 14 Ljupco/iStock/Getty Images Plus/Getty Images; p. 15 MediaNews Group/Orange County Register via Getty Images/Contributor/MediaNews Group/Getty Images; p. 18 Anadolu Agency/Contributor/Getty Images; p. 19 The Washington Post/Contributor/Getty Images; pp. 20, 21 Owen Humphreys - PA Images/Contributor/PA Images/Getty Images.

Some of the images in this book illustrate individuals who are models. The depictions do not imply actual situations or events.

Library of Congress Cataloging-in-Publication Data

Names: Rogers, Marie, 1990- author.
Title: Monster trucks / Marie Rogers.
Description: New York : PowerKids Press, 2022. | Series: Let's ride! | Includes index.
Identifiers: LCCN 2020045813 | ISBN 9781725327474 (library binding) | ISBN 9781725327450 (paperback) | ISBN 9781725327467 (6 pack) | ISBN 9781725327481 (ebook)
Subjects: LCSH: Monster trucks—Juvenile literature.
Classification: LCC TL230.15 .R645 2022 | DDC 629.224–dc23
LC record available at https://lccn.loc.gov/2020045813

Manufactured in the United States of America

CPSIA Compliance Information: Batch #CSPK22. For Further Information contact Rosen Publishing, New York, New York at 1-800-237-9932.

Find us on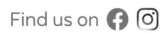

CONTENTS

AMAZING MONSTER TRUCKS

Have you ever seen a pickup truck with huge tires? If so, you've seen a monster truck! Monster trucks appear at shows and **perform** for crowds. They can be driven up and over large objects. These trucks can even be driven up on top of cars to crush, or flatten, them. Monster trucks also fly over big jumps.

Monster trucks are loud and powerful. Lots of people enjoy watching them crush big objects. Sometimes, the trucks even roll over!

Monster Jam is one of the biggest monster truck events. This **series** of live shows happens all over the world!

5

MAKING A MONSTER

Some people take regular pickup trucks and turn them into monster trucks. However, most of the monster trucks seen in big shows are specially made. Builders start by making a strong frame out of steel tubes, or pipes. The builders also put in large engines and supersized **shock absorbers**.

Then the builders add giant wheels and tires with huge treads, or lines, in them. Using controls called gears, drivers can steer, or direct, all four wheels separately.

MONSTERJAM.COM

Tires on monster trucks are 66 inches (168 cm) high and 43 inches (109 cm) wide.

LIVELY TRUCKS

The most famous monster trucks have colorful paint jobs and interesting names. Bigfoot and Grave Digger are two well-liked monster trucks. These trucks are both so popular that people have built many **versions** of them.

Some monster trucks have cool **designs**, like flames, painted on them. Others have pictures of animals. Some take it a step further and become animals! They often have eyes, mouths, and noses painted on. Some even have ears and tails coming out from the truck.

This monster truck is made to look like the TV dog Scooby-Doo. Check out the tail and ears coming out from the truck!

IN CONTROL

Driving a monster truck isn't an easy task. Drivers commonly sit in the middle of their monster trucks. The seats are made special for their bodies. The driver uses a steering wheel to turn the front wheels and a control called a switch to turn the back wheels.

When a truck crashes, the driver uses a switch called a kill switch to turn off the engine. Safety officials can also kill the engine if the driver isn't able to reach their switch.

A **harness** holds the driver in the seat, even while they do tricky moves.

A BIGFOOT BEGINNING

In the 1970s, a man named Bob Chandler added big wheels and **axles** to his pickup truck. He named the truck Bigfoot. It was so powerful, Chandler could drive Bigfoot over cars! Soon, Chandler was crushing cars in front of crowds.

As the sport grew, more and more events popped up, and more people came to watch the big trucks race, jump, and crash. In 1988, the Monster Truck Racing Association was formed to create official rules for the sport.

It didn't take long for monster truck shows to get big. Today, people fill **stadiums** to see the trucks fly through the air, crash, and more!

13

PART OF A TEAM

Behind every great monster truck is a great team. The team is made up of the owner, the driver, and **mechanics**. Sometimes, the owner is the driver. Teams travel with trailers, or big, wheeled objects pulled by a truck or car. These trailers hold the monster truck, extra truck parts, and tools.

Since so much force is put on monster trucks, they break down easily. Axles bend or break, and shock absorbers are destroyed. The tools and extra parts are used to fix these problems.

This is Dawn Creten. She's the driver of Scarlet Bandit, the monster truck shown behind her.

THE RACE IS ON!

Lots of people love watching monster truck shows. The main event usually features a race over a course filled with things to jump over. Some courses have cars that the trucks drive over and crush. Others have dirt jumps or sticky mud, called mud bogs.

Some monster truck races are timed. Each truck goes one at a time. In other races, two trucks race at once. The first to finish moves on to another round until there's only one winner!

You never know what will happen at a monster truck show. Sometimes the trucks go up on two wheels, jump, or flip over.

FREESTYLE TIME!

Another fan favorite at a monster truck show is the freestyle event. In the early 1990s, freestyle events became popular as a way for trucks that had lost races to keep performing during shows.

In a freestyle event, trucks go all over the course, jumping, crushing cars, and spinning around quickly. As long as the drivers follow safety rules, they can do pretty much anything they want. The crowds love when the drivers push the trucks so far they break or crash.

In addition to big shows like Monster Jam, monster trucks sometimes perform at local fairs.

79

MONSTER TRUCK MADNESS

Monster truck shows are some of the biggest touring, or traveling, shows in the world. Event series like Monster Jam put on races and freestyle events across the world. Crowds at these shows get to see some of the coolest monster trucks crush cars, spin doughnuts, and race.

Monster truck owners are always pushing the limits of what these **vehicles** can do. As trucks are built to be even more powerful, they'll go faster, jump higher, and pull off cooler tricks than ever before!

This monster truck wows fans at a show in England.

GLOSSARY

axle: A pin or bar that wheels rotate around.

design: The pattern or shape of something.

harness: A set of straps fitted to a person to keep them in place.

mechanic: A person who builds and fixes machines.

perform: To put on a show for a group of people.

series: A set of related things or events that are planned.

shock absorber: A part on a vehicle that makes a ride less bumpy.

stadium: A large, often roofless building used for events that has an open area surrounded by rows of seats.

vehicle: An object that moves people from one place to another.

version: A form of something that is different from others.

FOR MORE INFORMATION

BOOKS

Doeden, Matt. *Monster Trucks*. North Mankato, MN: Capstone Press, 2019.

Mikoley, Kate. *Monster Trucks*. New York, NY: Gareth Stevens Publishing, 2020.

WEBSITES

Are Monster Trucks Scary?
wonderopolis.org/wonder/are-monster-trucks-scary
Find out more about monster trucks here.

Monster Jam
www.monsterjam.com/en-US
Check out the official Monster Jam website to stay up-to-date on the latest happenings, watch videos, and learn more about the event.

INDEX